WOW!!! Finally, someone has captured the essence of authenticity. Judi Mason has gone deeper into the real meaning of "self discovery." I highly recommend *The Best Self Chronicles* to begin your journey of self worth, self value and self awareness!

—*Tonette Underwood,*
Broadcast & PR Professional

The Best Self Chronicles catapults the reader into a new way of thinking and living, designed to fulfill your purpose and destiny in life! This book is an injection of vitality, knowledge and power for the reader with mundane thoughts for tomorrow. What a masterful way of summing up the Chronicles series. Judi Mason has done it again!

—*Lisa Claiborne,*
Author & Entrepreneur

Judi's inspiration is medicinal. Each morning, I reach for her uplifting words to begin my day. She delivers clearly-written and very relatable nourishment that makes my soul smile. I hope I can find a seat in her workshops!

—*Sonia Storbeck,*
Sales Professional & Entreprenuer

The Best Self Chronicles is an excellent thought provoking read, which calls the reader to embark on a journey of self discovery, to becoming their best self.

—*Dr. Courtney A. Hammonds,*
Image Architect - Build. Educate. Style

The Best Self Chronicles

Rediscover, Reconnect, Reinvent YOU!

Judi Mason

DIVA Ink Publishers
Atlanta, Georgia

The Best Self Chronicles
Copyright © 2013 Judi Mason

For further information please contact:
Judi Mason by visiting www.judimason.com
or write to the office of Judi Mason

P.O. Box 7394
Atlanta, GA 30357
Email: info@judimason.com

Layout & Design: Susan L. Volkert
Editing: Scott Roberts

Library of Congress Control Number: 2013933316
Printed in the United States of America
ISBN: 978-0-9858625-1-0

All rights are reserved. No part of this publication may be reproduced or transmitted in any form or by any means, electronic or mechanical, including photocopying, recording or by any information storage and retrieval system, without the prior written permission of the author, except for the inclusion of brief quotations in a review.

Contents

Preface..ix
Introduction..xiii
My Story..3
Are You Living Your Dream?....................................9
What Is Your Excuse?...15
It's Never Too Late..21
Are You The Next Billionaire?................................29
What Are You Waiting For?...................................35
Will The Real You Please Come Forward?...........41
Revive & Renew Your Spirit..................................47
Age Ain't Nothing But A Number.........................53
Why Aren't You Fearless?......................................59
What Is Your Real Worth?.....................................65
Love & Encouragement Challenge........................69
Stick To The Plan...75
Life Agenda...81
Chloe Mantra...87
Empowered to Empower.......................................93
Rediscover You...97

Preface

In 2010 when I sat down to write *The Chloe Chronicles: Life Lessons I Learned From My Cocker Spaniel*, I was clueless about writing, publishing, and being an author. Now two years later, one book has turned into a three-book series, speaking engagements, workshops and seminars. When I started I was pursuing what I believe to be my purpose, so how appropriate that the focus of the third and final book in the Chronicle series is on pursuing your purpose and becoming your best self.

This writing journey has afforded me the opportunity to incorporate three core elements of becoming your best self:

Rediscovering:
A journey of self discovery—*The Chloe Chronicles*

Reconnecting:
Defining your true desires—*The Relationship Chronicles*

Reinventing:
Life application—*The Best Self Chronicles*

As you can see, each phase has a corresponding book in the

Chronicle series that helps bring a portion of each element to life. I am a firm believer that we have one life and that we should live it to the fullest, and the *Chronicles* series allows you to do just that. By helping individuals begin the discovery process of reconnecting with themselves. Each book is filled with an array of real-life principles and testimonials of real-life applications that will help readers develop and implement changes in their own lives.

I can't thank you enough for the overwhelming support of the books in the *Chronicle* series. My prayer is that they empower you to live life to the fullest and become your best authentic self. I wish you much success in your endeavors.

Judi

> "*It* takes courage to grow up and become who you really are."
> — *E. E. Cummings*

Introduction

At a young age, we were taught to go to school, get a job, retire, and live happily ever after; this was the prescription of the American dream. But nowhere in this prescribed formula does anyone take time to ask if this is the life path that we really want to pursue. Just because this worked for some, it does not mean that it works for everyone. Today our childhood dreams of saving the world have been replaced with PTA meetings, deadlines, after-school programs, and attempts to stay relevant in an ever-changing world.

We have become so engulfed in our self-absorbed drama that we neglect to be kind to a stranger or lend a helping hand to someone in need. We often ask ourselves, "who have I become?" Like most people, you need to detox and take a break from the drama and trauma of life and reconnect with **who you really are** today. Rediscover your passion, your dreams, and your desires. Embark on a personal journey of self-discovery to find new direction at this juncture in your life. I believe that this book will help you jump-start your journey of self-discovery.

For approximately two years, I was a featured author with

a weekly column for an online magazine; the chapters in this book are a compilation of my most popular articles regarding the pursuit of purpose. I hope you will allow these articles to help you begin a journey of self-discovery; reconnecting with your true desires and creating the life you imagined you would live.

I understand that it is so much easier to embark on a journey with someone else rather than going at it alone. That is the reason I always end my articles with an endearing remark such as "with love," because I believe that we are on this journey together. We are always evolving, growing, and changing. May this book inspire you in this next phase of your life's journey. Remember you are not alone; I'm right there with you.

Much success!

Judi

> *"It's* never too late to be what you might have been."
> — *George Elliot*

𝓑ACK IN 1997 I KNEW my career path would be that of a writer. At the time, I hadn't written a thing. I had no desire to write and to be honest, I was intimidated by the process and afraid that I would fail. So I ran. I attempted to dabble in writing but for the most part, it was too much for me and I pursued my own desires: music, marketing, public relations, cooking, ANYTHING but writing. In 2004 I started an online dessert bar-bistro called Fat & Healthy, specializing in gourmet desserts and entrees. Cooking is truly my passion and although I was in my zone, I still was not operating at my full potential. In 2009 a dear friend asked me to consider becoming a featured author for an online magazine. I accepted the invitation, not thinking much of it. Little did I know that my weekly column would help me develop a gift that I ran from for 12 years. In addition, it would ignite a desire in me to fulfill the call of writing, motivational speaking, and consulting.

I don't know what God has called you to do, but don't be like me and run. Embrace it. Yes it is scary! Yes, it is something new. And no, you are not in control. But God loves you. And He knows what is best for you. **Ironically, what you are running from will be the thing that you will love the most and end up running to.** I can attest to that.

I closed my dessert bar May 1, 2010. I published my first book, *The Chloe Chronicles: Life Lessons I Learned From My Cocker Spaniel*, November 15, 2010, I published my second book, *The Relationship Chronicles: Straight Talk, Real Love, No Drama!* on July 3, 2012 and I completed this book *The Best Self Chronicles: Rediscover, Reconnect, Reinvent YOU!* on November 19, 2012 and I have been writing ever since.

Join me and fulfill the destiny that God has for your life. No longer running from, but running to; no longer allowing the failures and mistakes of the past to hinder you from fulfilling your God-given purpose. Try again. I promise you will succeed.

Thank you for supporting my purpose. Now it's time for you to pursue yours!

With love,

Judi

What's your story?

Are You Living Your Dream?

As we grow up, we have visions and dreams of grandeur for our family, finances, careers, and our future. However, those dreams quickly fade away once the reality of life appears. We sometimes allow the challenges of life to take us down a path most traveled and we forget about our dreams and aspirations.

Today, I would like to challenge you to dream again! I challenge you to choose to pursue and live your dream. Open your mind to the possibilities that are ahead of you. Make a conscientious choice that you are going to live every day of your life to the fullest. How would you answer the following questions:

- What do you value most in life?
- Today, what are the three most important goals in your life?
- If you only had six months to live, how would you spend your time?
- What have you always wanted to do, but were just afraid to try?
- What activities bring you the most joy and a sense of accomplishment?
- Imagine if you were granted one wish, what would it be?

- What would you do if you hit the lottery and won a million dollars tax free tomorrow?

After answering these questions, can you honestly say that your current goals and activities mirror your true desires? Why or why not? I challenge you to make the necessary life changes that will allow you to live your dream and enjoy your life.

Work on yourself. You are your greatest asset or worst liability. – John Maxwell

Much love,

Judi

*A*re you living your dream?

What Is Your Excuse?

I WATCHED FOR THE MILLIONTH TIME the movie, *The Wedding Date*. During a discourse in the movie, a statement was made by the lead male character that a woman has the exact love life that she wants. Of course an argument ensued, but the foundation of his theory was that if a woman was unhappy with her love life, she had the power to change it.

The discourse made me think about people in general. If people want something better, then they need to make the necessary changes to do better. After all it is our choice. We are where we are today because of the choices we made yesterday be it good, bad, or indifferent. Some are trapped from the pain of a broken heart, disappointment, fear, etc., and based on those feelings, they have limited themselves and not chosen accordingly.

I would like to invite you to make a new choice to dream again. As you open yourself to the possibilities, consider the following questions:

- What would you do if you had unlimited resources?
- If nothing stood in your way, what would you really do?
- Remove your glass ceiling. What does that look like for you?
- Allow yourself the freedom to dream again, to believe

again, to hope again. What are the end results?
- ◦ Write down your dream list.
- ◦ Every day you get up, pursue your dream. How will you accomplish this exercise?
- ◦ The only thing in your way is you. Do you believe that to be true?

As you begin to ponder the answer to these questions, take the limits off and envision the endless possibilities.

Take the limits off! Release your hold and allow God to do what HE wants to do in your life. **Imagine a life with NO LIMITS! NO BOUNDARIES! WALK THROUGH YOUR OPEN DOOR!** Dare to dream again! See you on the other side of victory!

Much love,

Judi

What are your excuses?

It's Never Too Late...

$\mathcal{O}$KAY, NO MORE EXCUSES! So often, we hear that age is nothing but a number. While that is true, at the same time, we evaluate our accomplishments in life based on the goals and expectation that we set for ourselves by a certain age. Consciously and subconsciously, we use our age as a barometer to measure how successful we have or have not become in life. Our age-related goals are often set as follows: married by the age of 25; 2.5 children by 30; retired and living in a beachfront condo in the Caribbean at 65. We all know the drill. But here is the reality: When life does not happen as planned, we begin to take inventory. Some of us figure out a way to reinvent ourselves and others decide to stay at status quo, letting their hopes and dreams fade away. For those of you, who find yourselves at one end or the other, and even somewhere in between, let me share a story with you.

I am a foodie; as such my television is constantly on the Food Network. I am always looking for new recipes and creative presentation ideas, so naturally I am lured in by the decadent dishes highlighted on the various food shows. Aside from their culinary talents, the personal stories of the celebrity chefs are extremely interesting. One story that amazes me is Paula Deen a 65-year old Southern cook in Savannah, Georgia, who started her business out of a need.

"Newly divorced and with only $200 to her name, 42-year-old Paula packed up her two sons and moved from Albany, Georgia to Savannah. There she started her own catering business called The Bag Lady, where she prepared fresh lunches to sell to downtown businesses and doctors' offices."

I am sorry to interrupt, but did they say she started her business at the age of 42?

Sorry, I digress. Continue… "In 1990, Paula opened her own restaurant in the south side Savannah Best Western. Called The Lady and Sons, it served breakfast, lunch, and dinner in a small space that could seat 42 people maximum. The restaurant remained in that location for four years, where Paula and her sons built their business with a core of faithful patrons. In 1995 Paula jumped on the opportunity to relocate to downtown Savannah, where The Lady and Sons has been ever since." (From Paula Deen's bio on www.foodnetwork.com)

At an age when most people are getting their second wind in life, Paula Deen was just getting started. At the time, no one knew Paula Deen suffered from panic attacks and agoraphobia—a phobia which causes people to stay at home because they can't face the fears of what might happen in the real world. Due to her condition, she had to do something to make a living and provide for her family, so she turned to what she knew: cooking. Many of us have chosen career paths that we may like or even enjoy but in essence, it is not really our passion. Like Paula Deen, we had to do something in order to survive.

Now 23 years later at the tender age of 65, with the help of her 10-year stint on Food Network, not only has Paula Deen faced her demons, but she has remarried and built an empire under the Paula Deen brand. Her empire includes a number of endorsements, an extensive product line of food, books, magazines, television shows, and appearances. Also under her umbrella, her brother Bubba Deen, her sons Jamie and Bobby Deen, and her husband Michael Groover have all established their personal brands.

It has been said that when you walk out your destiny and purpose, you touch so many people's lives, and Paula Deen is an excellent example of that. By Paula Deen operating in survival mode and doing what she knew how to do, she opened the door to so many in her immediate family and beyond. Not only did her sons benefit but they were able to offer stardom to others. While taping a segment of their show *Road Tasted with Jamie and Bobby*, they discovered a couple from Memphis, Tennessee—Pat and Gina Neely, co-owners of Neely's barbecue. They fell in love with the Neelys and helped pave the way for the Neelys to join the Food Network family. And boy did they ever. The Neelys took Food Network by storm.

"After its February 2008 premiere, *Down Home with the Neelys* became the highest-rated series debut in the five-year history of Food Network's "In the Kitchen" weekend block and continues to be a top ratings performer. Filmed in their Memphis home surrounded by family and friends, the show airs seven days a week on Food Network. The Neelys launched a second Food Network show in July 2008, *Road Tasted with the Neelys*, a cross-country search for specialty stores and family-run businesses that make hand-crafted, one-of-a-kind edibles. In May 2009, the Neelys released their first cookbook entitled *Down Home with the Neelys* (Knopf, 2009), which quickly earned a place on the New York Times' best-seller list." (From Pat & Gina Neely's bio www.foodnetwork.com)

Wow! The Neelys just needed an opportunity. They were prime and ready when opportunity knocked on their door.

Question: Who is waiting on you to show up to catapult them into their destiny?

Better yet, **who are you waiting on to open the door to your next opportunity?** If they showed up today, would you be ready? That is an excellent question: Are you ready? Do you know your purpose? Can you articulate it? Have you made the necessary moves to walk in your destiny? If not, what's hindering you? Are you looking at your past failures, your circumstances, your age? Truth be told, most people are hindered by their age coupled with past failures more than anything else. Some feel that they are too young and that no one will take them seriously or they feel that they are too old and that no one will take them seriously. Either way, they allow something as minute as a number to hinder them from their destiny.

Well today decide: **NO MORE EXCUSES!** There is too much work to be done and there are too many people waiting on you to show up. Age is just a number. You are never too young or too old to get started. It's not too late or too soon to pursue your passion and dreams. So many people are waiting on you. You are the key to their destiny and they are the key to yours.

"Who would think that Paula Deen, a housewife from Albany, Georgia, with no formal training in food, would become one of the country's most beloved celebrity chefs?" (From Paula Deen bio on www.foodnetwork.com)

Paula Deen showed up and did what needed to be done out of necessity. She has not only prospered but has afforded others to be able to do the same. All you have to do is show up and do what you know how to do. And God will do the rest. Give God an opportunity to allow His favor to shine on you. Give Him something to work with. Give Him something to bless. The best is yet to come.

Here is to your success! Remember we win.

Much love,

Judi

P.S. If you need a little more inspiration, look at a portion of the product line that 65-year-old Paula Deen has been able to amass.

According to the Paula Deen store at www.pauladeen.com her empire consists of the following:

- ✓ Books
- ✓ Calendars
- ✓ Cookbooks
- ✓ Cookware
- ✓ Furniture
- ✓ Magazines
- ✓ Reading Glasses
- ✓ Seafood
- ✓ Spices, Mixes, Sauces
- ✓ Sweets

What dream did you let go of?
Finish this sentence: It's not too late to...

Are You The Next Intentional Billionaire?

AFTER VIEWING THE MOVIE *SOCIAL NETWORK*, I was in awe. The movie is based on of the book, The Accidental Billionaire by Ben Mezrichs. The story is about the success of Facebook and its founder, Mark Zuckerberg. According to the movie, accidental is exactly what Zuckerberg's success was. His need to create Facebook was not out of a desire to make money but a desire to improve his social status. His diligence and wherewithal to see the project through to the end is what brought about his success. Because he was focused on a project that he was passionate about and put in the needed work to bring it alive, today he is ranked the youngest billionaire in the world. Although there are conflicting reports regarding the authenticity of the book and the movie be it truth or fiction, the fact remains that Facebook exists and has been a phenomenal success.

My question to you:

If Zuckerberg was able to accomplish his current status by accident, what can you accomplish on purpose? Will you be the next INTENTIONAL billionaire? It is not a hard goal to strive for—just abandon all doubt and fear and pursue your passion and STRIVE for success!

The key is that you **choose to pursue your passion.** Once you determine your passion, set up and establish a firm foundation to launch from. It is never too late to be successful. You haven't missed it. It's not too late! As a matter of fact, you are right on time! Why not start today?

Remember you will succeed!

With love,

Judi

What are you passionate about?
What do you love to do or
desire to see changed?

What Are You Waiting For?

When you meditate on the word of God you reset the boundaries in your life. God didn't set the boundaries that you have in your life, you did! - Bill Winston

During a recent visit to a convenience store, three men in their 40's were standing in the middle of the store discussing "the man." How creative and prosperous "the man" was and how "the man" knew how to make money, etc. I left the store livid. I could not understand how three able-bodied men could proclaim the success of someone else but not for a moment think that they could create their own opportunity for wealth. I was speechless. After leaving the store, I heard a song by hip hop mogul Jay Z entitled "Encore" playing on the radio; the next thing I heard was the chorus:

What are you waiting for?

At that moment, I wanted to run back in the store and SCREAM:

What are you waiting for!

I don't know the story of these men. But their confession of hopelessness and destitution was depressing. After researching the lyrics to the song "Encore", I realized that Jay Z is sharing his trials and struggles of making it to the top of his industry. In this song, he speaks about the dues that he had to pay, how his record company didn't believe in him, but through it all, he made it. The verse that caught my attention:

And I need you to remember one thing (one thing): I came, I saw, I conquered from record sales, to sold out concerts.

I like this verse because Jay Z made an effort to fulfill his dream. He showed up. Not only did he show up, but he conquered, he succeeded and in the end, he won.

This song reminds me of a book by T.D. Jakes entitled: *Repositioning Yourself: Living Life Without Limits*. This book deals with the subject of reinventing yourself. We often get lost in the monotony of life. At those moments, we need to take time to reconnect with our true selves and rediscover our purpose while recreating the path to our new-found destiny. By gaining a new perspective, we are able to stay focused on the task at hand.

During this time of discovery, take a look in the mirror and ask yourself:

What have you been waiting for?

Sending hugs & love your way,

Judi

What have you been waiting for? What will it take to get you to move forward regarding the things that you desire?

Will the Real You Please Come Forward?

"Don't let life discourage you; everyone who got where he is had to begin where he was." - Richard L. Evans

Like most, I welcome each day with open arms. The wonderful possibilities, the newness of life, the smell of overwhelming optimism and the vision of endless opportunities represent the exhilarating prospects that are always so intoxicating about a new day.

I think as individuals, we have done a great job of making sure everyone else has been taken care of, from our employer to our family and everyone and everything in between. However, somewhere in the hustle and bustle of life, we forgot to take care of ourselves. I challenge you to turn your attention and focus inward. Make sure that you take time to enjoy your life. Evaluate your current state:

- Are you enjoying life?
- Are you participating in activities that you enjoy?
- Are the people around you (family, friends, associates) encouraging you to be the best YOU that you can be?

Decide to make and implement the necessary lifestyle changes in an effort to always put yourself first.

I am sure a lot of you are clueless on how and where to begin. Let's start by revamping your daily routine. Try adding some exciting adventure or activity into your life. Better yet, foster new relationships by going out and meeting like-minded people who are interested in the same activities. Just take time and think outside the box. Introduce yourself to something new.

Whatever area that you find yourself lacking or missing that "thrill" in, make an effort to introduce yourself to a NEW array of choices. Remember there is always someone out there that likes to do what you like to do. You just have to take time to find them.

I believe that as you venture out of your routine, you will rediscover who you really are and what you really like to do. And possibly decide to rekindle your hopes, dreams, and passion. Take time out this year, this month, right now, to get to know you again.

Reintroduce yourself to the new YOU. I think they have been waiting to meet each other for a very long time. Have fun! Live Life to the fullest!

Much love,

Judi

Who are you really?

Not the person that is so organized and is a perfect employee. No, who are YOU. The real you. What are your real dreams and aspirations? Who are you today in this very moment?

Revive
And Renew
Your Spirit

WHAT IS DISTRACTING YOU? So often the cares of life—work, family, activities, etc.—keep us so busy that at the end of the day, we don't remember anything that we did. We are always in a hurry and if the truth be told; 90% of the time, we are really not going anywhere. Between the cell phone, emails, text messages, social media, meetings, reports, deadlines, errands, household duties, attempting a social life, as well as other activities, when do you have time for yourself? Better yet, where does your time with God fit in? Distractions such as these will force you to get off course.

I am known as a true multitasker and when I am not doing a million things at once my friends swear that something is wrong. I am guilty of rushing through one task to get to another, all in an effort to complete my mental to do list. Recently while reviewing such a list, I realized that I had not set aside time to spend with God. For me, that was a problem.

As I started to conduct a mental inventory of my week, quiet, committed and dedicated time set aside for just me and God had not occurred. The only quiet time I had given God was in the morning, when I rolled over in bed and said, "Good morning, Lord," and at night when I laid down in bed. I immediately asked for forgiveness. I was so busy working the blessings that had been bestowed upon me that I was not spending time praising and thanking the One who gave them to me.

For me, spending time with God is an honor. When you really take time to talk to the Lord, you are overwhelmed by His love and not the challenges of your day. It is a time of real communion and fellowship with God. A time where I am renewed, I am strengthened, encouraged, and most of all filled with the peace and tranquility of His presence.

As you spend time resting in God, in meditation and prayer, things in your life seem to line up. Make a commitment today to make God a priority and schedule a date with Him daily. You need it! Trust me!

Have a wonderful week,

Judi

What are some ways that you can revive, refresh and renew your spirit?

Age Ain't Nothing But A Number

"There is so much talk about 40 being the new 20. Maybe people feel that way because they just turned 40. It appears that when a person enters their 40s, there is a new lease on life. It's like these individuals begin to once again embrace the freedom and liberation that they possessed in their 20s. They feel as if they have been set free. The free spirit within is finally unleashed. They no longer second-, third-, or fourth-guess themselves on matters that are true to them. They finally give themselves permission to live. So many 40-somethings are rediscovering life, love, and themselves in a new way.

No matter what age, every age is a great age. You are forever maturing, growing, learning, and discovering who you really are. In your 20s, you are trying to figure out what to do now that you are officially a grown-up. In your 30s, you are really coming into your own. You start pulling back the layers and really start finding yourself. I think in your 30s, you begin to settle within yourself exactly who you are and where you are going.

In your 40s, you have discovered and become one with the real you, and you are ready to conquer the world! When you are 50+, you are living YOUR life. You do and say what you want; who is going to stop you? You have officially earned the right.

No matter your age, enjoy every day as if it were your last! Live on purpose!

My mantra: Do You! Be You! Free You!

Much love!

Judi

Freedom to be you.
What does that mean to you?

Why Aren't You Fearless?

*D*URING A MEETING, fearlessness really smacked me in the face. When we were younger, be it in our teen years, 20s, 30s, or just yesterday, most of us were fearless. We did what needed to be done without a second thought. We stepped out without a security blanket, because we just knew that we would succeed. Then the inevitable happened – LIFE! A few challenges in life knocked a lot of people's tenacity right out the window. Those who were once fearless became fearful. Life has thrown all of us a few hard punches and in some cases, instead of getting better, it has knocked us out. Today, I challenge you no matter what curveball life has thrown you, GET UP! Be that fearless overcomer you use to be. And if you never were fearless, it's never too late to reinvent yourself.

"The greatest glory in living lies not in never falling, but in rising every time we fall." - Nelson Mandela

With God behind you, you cannot lose; you learn and you grow. And that is truly the best place to be. I have lost a lot over the years from material possessions to loved ones but in spite of it all, through the hurt, the pain, and disappointments, God has sustained me and I am still here. I realized that I have to choose to walk through the challenges of life to the very end.

People will leave and challenges will occur but when life hands you metaphorical lemons, make strawberry lemonade. I have learned to change my perspective and my perception. Either the glass is half empty and I focus on what I don't have or what has happened to me OR it's half full, and I focus on where I am going and the potential that awaits me. I realized that the choice is mine. And the choice is yours too. With God on our side, no matter the outcome we are victorious.

> *"I can do all things, through Christ who strengthens me."*
> *(Philippians 4:13)*

Join me on this life journey. Let's get that tenacious fearlessness back, coupled with the right boundaries and limits that force us to be the AWESOME people we were destined to become.

Much love,

Judi

How can you be fearless?

What do you need to do to become fearless?

What Is Your Real Worth?

A DEAR FRIEND POSTED THIS QUESTION on her Facebook page and it has been a true character test.

If your character is your currency, how much are you worth? –Anonymous

Whatever the value, you can always increase your denomination. Come up higher.

You are valuable!

Judi

What is your value?
What is your worth?

An OLD FRIEND FOUND ME on Facebook, and as he read over my information tab, he was so excited about the various endeavors that I am pursuing that he picked up the phone to share his support and encouragement. I can't begin to tell you how that made my day. I don't think that I stopped smiling the entire day. Sometimes we just need a random act of kindness to encourage us on our journey. A little appreciation goes a long way.

I would like to challenge you to encourage others on their journey. Beginning this week, make an effort to reach out to not only those in your immediate circle, but to old friends that you have lost contact with, coworkers, associates, and even strangers. Let them know how much you appreciate them. Let them know you care. Show them some love and encourage them in their endeavors.

Are you up for the challenge?

I am! Let me be the first to show my appreciation.

I would like to thank each of you for purchasing this book. Your support encourages me to continue writing. My prayer is that this book is a blessing to you. May the words offer

helpful insight and may they touch your life in a meaningful way. ♥

See, it is just that easy. Now it is your turn to show some love.

Spread the love!

Judi

Acts of Kindness:
To whom can you show your love and appreciation?

When I initially saw the movie *The Book of Eli* I had no idea what the movie was about. I didn't recall seeing a full trailer, so I was going on blind faith of reviews from friends and associates. The first viewing was a matinee in an empty theater. The second viewing was a Saturday night in a packed house. I believe I needed to see it in silence the first time in order to appreciate it in concert. At the end of the movie, people applauded, something that I have not heard in a long time. I walked away with a feeling of conviction and inspiration.

This movie showed me so much about myself. Especially how I take so many things for granted; how arrogantly I expect the luxuries of life to always be here. And more so than ever, how I do not appreciate the gift that God has given us – His Word (the Bible). As believers, we are so busy quoting scriptures and telling others about themselves that we often don't take time to check ourselves. When do we ever sit down and really appreciate the beauty of the words in the Bible? The poetic movements of the Psalms, the whimsical irony of Proverbs, the painful and delicate truth of the Gospels, the historical context of the Old Testament, or the road map to life in the New Testament. The Bible is a book that has just become words that we claim to live by but not words that we

REALLY appreciate and take to heart.

The Book of Eli convicted and inspired me to continue on the journey that the Lord has set before me no matter the obstacles, the challenges, or the dangers. *Eli* had a mantra that we should all adopt:

Stay focused and stay on the path

Eli's mantra reminds me of Jeremiah 29:11

For I know the thoughts that I think toward you, says the LORD, thoughts of peace and not of evil, to give you a future and a hope.

God has chosen us for a purpose. He will lead and guide us, if we will listen to His leading. He will guide our way clearly. We all have a destiny to fulfill on this earth. God has entrusted a particular task to each of us. **We have to be careful not to get so caught up in reaching the destination that we don't appreciate the journey.**

This film is very powerful and inspiring. The overall message that I left with was never give up on what God has chosen you to do. You might have detoured; you might have fallen off the path, but get up! You are truly able to accomplish what has been set before you. This isn't just for you; so many are waiting on you to complete the task at hand.

Remember, we win! God Bless.

Much love,

Judi

What do you need to do to stay focused and stick to the plan?

I DON'T KNOW ABOUT YOU, but I think the time seems to be flying by. It seems like I blinked and the year is passing me by. I think one of the reasons I feel this way is that I was so busy trying to handle life, that I am not sure I took time out to actually live it. I can't honestly say that I enjoyed or at least appreciated each day that was given to me. And for that reason, if nothing else, I have to make sure that I handle today and beyond differently.

In an effort to do better and make substantial changes, I was challenged to set life goals. By creating a personal development plan that includes the following:

- Highlight at least five key areas that you want to improve.
- Under each specified area, highlight what you would like to improve and how you plan to accomplish your goal. Be strategic in setting your goals.
- Find an accountability partner that will help you stay focused and ensure your success.

One major key to your success is to ELIMINATE all negativity that attempts to surround you, including friends, situations, or circumstances. Surround yourself with positivity. If that means changing your crowd, doing things differently, or making a self-adjustment, do what needs to be done in order to usher peace and tranquility into your life.

Another key factor to your success is to be sure to decide and define who you are and what you are about. Write out your personal mission and vision statement each day and determine to pursue each with diligence.

Each morning we are given a clean slate to work with and for that I am grateful. Choose to celebrate those new opportunities by making the most out of each and every day. If you are as guilty as I am of not living life to the fullest, from this moment on, **CHOOSE** to **LIVE**, **ENJOY**, and **APPRECIATE** each day that you are given.

Let's choose to take the world by storm and enjoy our lives in the process.

I wish you much success!

Hugs & love,

Judi

Personal Development Plan

Chloe Mantra
Live, Love
& Enjoy Life

My first book is entitled *The Chloe Chronicles: Life Lesson's I Learned From My Cocker Spaniel*. My dog Chloe was a special dog who lived by her own set of rules. Just by her actions she became a four-legged life coach to everyone she encountered. In the book, I share the lessons that I learned from her. But the best lesson was how Chloe taught me how to live, love, and just enjoy life through the following lessons:

- Love unconditionally!

- Forgive immediately!

- Attempt to rectify an error or mistake instantly.

- Let go of an offense: IT'S NOT WORTH IT!!!!

- Play with those who want to play with you. Walk away from those who don't.

- Realize you can't force anyone to like or love you. If they are unable to see your worth, then they are obviously not worthy of you.

- Believe you are special! You are valuable! You are worthy! Accept it! Embrace it! Walk in it!

- Most of all, know that you are loved.

- Sow love and you will reap love.

I believe those are pretty good rules to live by. Much Success.

With love,

Judi

Live, love & enjoy life. How can this mantra become your reality?

THIS IS A GREAT EXAMPLE of what fulfilling your purpose looks like:

> "A difficult time can be more readily endured if we retain the conviction that our existence holds a purpose – a cause to pursue, a person to love, a goal to achieve."
> – **John Maxwell**

No matter what you endure in life, the lessons you learn, the things you discover, and the solutions you created are for you to share with others, so they won't have to walk the same path. We are empowered to empower others and that is what fulfilling your purpose is all about.

Let's continue to spread the love!

Judi

Who can you empower? And how will you empower them?

"Happiness is not something you postpone for the future; it is something you design for the present."
- Jim Rohn

I am sure that the chapters in this book have ignited or reignited your passion to pursue your dreams and purpose. Now, where do you begin? I would suggest that you take advantage of this momentum and begin a journey of self-discovery. Start with prayer seeking spiritual guidance and direction. Decide what you would like to pursue and then take time to plan and strategize your next move. Begin to plot and plan your aspirations and include them into your daily routine. Make it a part of your lifestyle so that it will become a part of who you are. All you need is the desire to live on purpose; as you make this a priority, it will then turn into a habit, which will prevent it from becoming a hobby.

I have always been taught that the most important part on your tombstone won't be when you were born or when you died but the dash in the middle. What did you do while you were here? Did you make an impact? Did you leave a mark that can't be erased? If you had to define the dash in the middle right now, would you be on target?

It's never too late to pursue your dreams and create your own success story. I did and I can honestly say that I am my Best Self. Allow yourself the ability to fall in love with your dreams again. Pursue them with everything within you. You will win. You will be victorious!

There is no greater joy than operating in your God ordained purpose. Stepping out in faith to pursue what you love can be scary, but as a Christian I have the love of Jesus Christ and the word of God (the Bible) guiding me along the way. If you would like to experience God's love and learn more about His word, visit: www.judimason.com/faith.

You will be successful. See you at the top!

Judi

P.S. If you need a little guidance in figuring out your purpose visit www.chazown.com. The exercises in this teaching will help you gain the insight you seek. Much success!

Thanks so much for your support! I hope you have enjoyed the *Chronicle* series. If you've missed any of the previous books be sure to visit: www.thechronicleseries.com

Let's stay connected via social media:
Stay in touch, join our mailing list:
www.judimason.com/contact

Follow Me on…
Twitter: twitter.com/judimason
Facebook: facebook.com/judimason.empowerment
Have a question? Email me at: judi@divaink.com

From my heart:
My sincere desire is for you to become the BEST YOU that you can be. Make every day count and choose to live on purpose.
Let's make YOUR DREAMS become a reality!

Much love,

Judi

Empowered to Empower Others

www.ingramcontent.com/pod-product-compliance
Lightning Source LLC
LaVergne TN
LVHW041631070426
835507LV00008B/563